A Collection of Memories in Times of Light & Dark

Gaurav Pichara

BookLeaf Publishing

Presentation by *BookLeaf Publishing*

Web: www.bookleafpub.com

E-mail: info@bookleafpub.com

ISBN : 9789357699419

First edition 2022

DEDICATION

I dedicate this book to my friends and family who guided me when all seemed lost. To my CH family and to the friends outside who pushed me to be my best, I sincerely Thank You All!

ACKNOWLEDGEMENT

I want to thank the people in my life who inspired me to write and gave me the strength to keep writing even when times seemed dark. To those who know me, I appreciate you all and I would not be where I am without you all behind me pushing & supporting me to get out of my comfort zone.

PREFACE

Most of the poems in this book are of events or feelings during events that happened in my life. They were experiences of my own. The timing of writing these poems were during special occasions or holidays, but also a few are romantic in nature. The combination of old school feelings and a wave of new experiences seen and heard make this book one of a kind. Although this book is written to face my own fears, I also hope that people can both get some entertainment as well as take away a couple of life lessons from here.

True Sight

A person who can't see, yet their sight is better than those who can. Issues that are grey, yet are defined by black and white. Nuance when taken out of context is a bigger threat than an invasion. A person who travels and learns, yet they do not belong. A nomad turned ghost yet they gain more wisdom than those who stay in one place. Roots must be strong, yet they must also be flexible. Yet, in the world today, a tree without roots is more learned than a tree with roots. Fluid as water, yet strong as fire. Experience of air with the age of a redwood. The nature of duality exists with mankind, yet wisdom of the universe seems to elude us.

Life

I've contemplated it many times before. Overwhelmed and screaming into the void. It doesn't help but who can we turn to when even those who we look to for help tell us to not think about it. When the void starts to stare back at us, we start becoming what we stared at. How can we not think about it when society tells us we MUST succeed or we are deemed as failures. We live in the age of too much information. Misinformation is deadlier than no information at all. It can lead to the death of individuals, of a loss of a family. Where do we turn to when all we have is misinformation and people who are ignorant and can't help. The gods have left us on a battlefield yet not everyone is a soldier or a warrior. So, how do we live, how do we survive? Can we survive in the first place when our skills are being deemed as either useless or not enough. The true end is not when our body collapses, but when we give up.

The Cost of Content and Piece of Mind

The dream of one who has many worries is one of peace. Yet at what price? Living in the space of emptiness. Yelling at the void. Facing the storm, both inside and out. What is the price of peace? Cost of sanity and the breakdown of the mind and soul. How far would one go down the route of madness? Is the price worth the peace?

Fall of Hero into Fear

This is about the fall of a man, of a hero. The master of audacity. The most daring, the boldest. The one who thinks outside the box. To most people, he is the man who knew no fear. But, fear lives inside him anyway. Chewing away at the walls of steel in his heart. Demons live everywhere. They are fought and defeated or they defeat people. But, inside of him lives a demon of another kind. The cold kind, cold as ice. One time in his childhood, he was on a playground. He remembered being bullied. Bullied because he was different, because he stood out. This is the kind of demon that lives inside his heart: the demon of those who bullied and made fun of him. Everyday, he wrestles with this icy demon. But, for all his strength, he can't push back. He's losing. And nothing can stop the cold dead voice that whispers in his mind, "you can't succeed". Everywhere he looked, he couldn't find an answer. But, the demon whispered to him. "Join with me. Become one with me and I'll help you find success. The success of money and power. The power of having the last laugh at those horrible kids." Not one scrap of lore or meditation helped him choke this demon. There was an answer. One he had for years, hidden from sight. He stopped. His agony evaporated. It was simple. All he had to do was decide what he wanted. Safety, peace, security. Again, the demon whispered, "come to me. Join with me." With one arm, he caught the demon and crushed away its voice. He broke its power with a single effortless twist. He decided then. He wouldn't just crush the demon. He would also take its power for his own. I am the master tactician and strategist. The general and writer who would inspire with my words and money. He ground the demon's corpse to dust beneath his heel. As he watched the demon's dust and ashes scatter before the blast of his furnace heart, he whispered "You, you are nothing. Nothing at all." He had finally become what they all called him, the man with no fear. This is his story. This is the story of the fear of the demon. After graduation, there was nothing. Nothing at all. No opportunities, no help, no support. Then, you remembered it all. The demon who brought forth this man of greed, the cold venom, the furnace in your heart, the darkness that seized everyone's helping hand. In one blazing moment in which you finally understood that there was no demon. There was no darkness. There was only you. That was all you, is you. Only you. When you could've been thinking about them. You were only thinking of yourself. Then you understood the final cruelty of life, because now, yourself is all you will ever have. You rage, scream and crush your insides. You remember all the dreams and hopes, all the power you once had. But, the power you can touch is only a memory. Now, the shadow is all you have left, because the shadow understands you, the shadow forgives you, the shadow gathers you into the heart of fire you have left, and within this furnace, you burn only yourself. This is how the hero with no fear fell into only fear.

The Impossible Journey of Approval

A child running after an impossible goal. He can see it, but he can never reach it. The goal is too distant, yet, he runs. He pursues it as a cat pursues the reflection of the moon in the water. Too far, yet it seems so close. He runs and runs, chasing it till the end. He screams while running, but he feels so far behind. He feels that he can't reach the end. A gate exists where there should be a door. The shadows pursuing him are his desires folding up. He can't seem to make it but he runs anyway. Even as he loses strength, his inner fire only grows everyday. He pursues his destination but the journey never ends.

Celestial & Happy Rakhi Pandaga

Thank you. Very sincerely, thank you. You were the moon to my earth. Even when times seemed dark, there was a ray. A ray of light that lit a path. The moon might not appear at times but it's always there. Looking over the earth. Watching it, guiding it, shining its light on it. Even though, it's so far, it can still influence the waves here. We wonder at its power. Yet even though, we think we know, it still has many things yet to show. They say time is a river. If the moon can influence that river, a sister has the power to influence time. Time with family, time with fun and time with you. Thank you! Wishing you a very Happy Rakhi Pandaga!

Happy Krishnashtami

Krishna. A name that brings both joy and devotion to the people. A man who was born a god. The eighth avatar of Lord Vishnu. A man who brought with him a child-like joy, yet a warrior king who no man could match on the other. Your power so great that you even decided not to fight in the Kurukshetra yudham. You brought hope to your people and through them to us. You who knows all yet who remains so humble as to not spread your teachings outright. Instead, you asked your greatest devotee Lord Bhishma to pass on your teachings in his final moments. Your inner child who can love everyone including your foes, qualities that we spend our entire lifetime to develop, you keep with no effort. Your humility is unbounded, your kindness is infinite, your teachings worth no less than this universe. A lord born without a throne, among simple cowherds yet who rose to call himself a king. A man born a god, but a god who calls himself a man. Happy Birthday Lord Krishna and Happy Krishnashtami to everyone!

Happy Vinayaka Chavithi

Lord Ganesh, you are the god of wisdom and intellect. You symbolize life and death. We appear one day and disappear another day. You who love durva, an invasive species, but one that takes nutrients but fertilizes the land. Ganesha, you have an elephant's head. An animal who can retain more information than any human could. Ganesh Chaturthi is a day to at least start striving to multiply our intelligence, not our bellies. A strong mind needs a strong body. People may say that you have a big belly but you have a bigger and stronger mind and it is those with the mental capability and sense who can bring out the best in not only themselves but in others around them. Thank you for teaching us this and Happy Birthday to you Lord Ganesha. And a Happy Ganesh Chaturthi and/or Vinayaka Chavithi. Jai Ganesha!

Happy Dasara & Navratri

Celebrating ten days of removing sin during Navratri, then the final day celebrating Dasara and Vijayadashami. The conquering of demons such as Mahishasura and Ravana. We celebrate these days but do we truly understand and live by them? These days are a reminder that we must conquer our own sins and fears, but we celebrate them by artificial means rather than live by them. The sins of Kama (lust), Krodha (anger), Moha (delusion), Lobha (greed), Mada (pride), Maatsyasya (envy), Manas (mind), Buddhi (intellect), Chitta (will) and Ahamkara (the ego) are in everyone but instead of trying to conquer them, we forget about them for these ten days. So, do we Really understand what we are celebrating? Both Ramudu and Durgamma were embodiments of Gods and Goddesses, but are they really special? They conquered their sins and lived life and became greater than humans. We can follow their example, but do we have the strength to? If they could do it, why can't we? Ramudu was a god born as a man. But, he lived with virtue and tried to set an example for us all. Durgamma was a goddess, but one who protected people who were in danger, especially women. So, why do women in modern life fear the fight for liberty and justice when a woman in the age of the Gods and Demons didn't. We must all follow the examples set by Rama, the Pandavas and Durgamma. Yudhishthir means one who is balanced in war state of mind or in dilemma [Yudh means war and isthir means balanced]. Yudhishthir indicate the quality of being balanced and static during any diversity or facing a problem. Arjuna indicates the focus quality of a person and Bheema represents the quality of inner strength. Nakul means to be neutral in life and Sahdeva means welfare of all. These people set the qualities of virtue, balance and living well in life. We must stride to become better ourselves and not just celebrate on a day. Happy Dasara and Vijayadashami to everyone!

Happy Holi

Holi. The Festival of Colors and the celebration of Good over Evil as well as the changing of seasons from Winter to Spring. A time for the community to come together again after the melting of ice and snow. The time to make bonfires and play with colors. The renewal of life through the exchange of holi gifts, snack hampers, dry fruits and greeting cards. Just as the spring colors start to emerge on the new leaves of trees, new opportunities and colors of life onto the streets. Red for love and fertility; yellow for the natural remedy turmeric; Green for new beginnings; and Blue for Krishna; Purple & Pinks for wealth and grandeur. Truly, a time for devotion to the world around us. A time to wash away our evils through the cleansing of our bodies in the waters afterwards and a time to pass the stories of our past around the bonfires at night. A time also for love and introspectiveness. May our fires be bright as the sun and our houses as welcoming as the new Spring! I wish everyone a very Happy Holi!

Happy Sankranti

Sankranti. A holiday where we celebrate the changing of the alignment and movement of the planet. Every time the zodiac sign changes, it is called Sankranti. Just as the planet moves, we understand the movement of human lives also. This holiday, we also celebrate the harvest and everything that went into it. A day for the planet, a day for people and a day for the animals and livestock. We celebrate the present and the coming of the future. Just as we celebrate the hard work of the farmers and livestock, we also celebrate the spiritual and celestial connections. The yogic system developed around the movement of both the human and celestial systems. Just as they change from moment to moment, we must also look to change and develop every moment. To understand change, we must understand stillness and this is the perfect time to do exactly that. "When a human being makes the necessary effort to touch the stillness within himself, only then he knows the joy of movement. Otherwise, people are bewildered by the movement of life. Every change that happens in their life they suffer." I'm wish every person a very happy and joyous Sankranti!

Happy Maha Shivaratri

Shivratri. A Hindu festival of many legends, stories and even origins. It is almost as old as the Ram Navami festival. One story is of Lord Shiva becoming the Neelakantha. Another story is where he stopped a conflict between Lords Brahma and Vishnu. Another story where Shiva took the form of a Linga. It is also celebrated as the anniversary of Lord Shiva and Goddess Parvati, when he wed her due to her devotion to him. She fasted for his good health after their marriage. Today also, this ritual is followed by an Indian woman who prays for the long life of their husbands. Not a destroyer, rather a balancer of good and evil. Only when evil takes over does his wrath appear. Those who follow Lord Shiva pray for moksha or the ending of their cycle of rebirth to rejoin the essence of the God himself. Several devotees pray the whole night, chant mantras in praise of Lord Shiva. It is also believed that those people who perform puja, fast, and offer prayers to Lord Shiva are blessed with good luck. To all those who follow the ways of Lord Shiva, I offer nothing but the happiest Shivratri. May your soul rejoin the essence of God at the end of this life!

Happy Ram Navami

Ram Navami, a holiday that is as old as the indus valley civilization itself. The celebration of the birth of the seventh avatar of Lord Vishnu - Lord Marayada Purshottam Ram himself. One of the most major holidays in the hindu community all over the world. A celebration of salvation itself as the royal family of Ayodhya finally had a successor to inherit the throne after the time of King Dasharatha. Not only the royal family but every resident of the place heaved a sigh of relief and thanked God for this miracle, little knowing that God himself was present among them in the form of Rama, the newborn son of Kausalya. It is also the end of the nine day Chaitra-Navratri celebrations. A day where all the devotees who fast are filled with endless happiness and good luck. The name Rama literally means someone who is divinely blissful and who gives joy to others, and one in whom the sages rejoice. On this day, a god was born and his reign in Ayodhya is referred to as Ramarajya, the epitome of perfect governance. We celebrate not only the brith, but also the reign of such a great man. A man born a god, but reigned as a King. A king who transcended to Godhood through his deeds. His life and achievement are celebrated every year. I wish all those who still follow his ways, the very happiest Ram Navami!

Happy Ugadi

A day marking the new year and a new spring. A chance to begin again, to grow out mindset just as we grow new crops. The Hindu holiday marks a new year as it follows the lunar calendar. Just as new leaves and new crops start to emerge, a chance for people to begin again appears. What better time and chance to worship Lords Brahma and Vishnu than the time of the spring. A time for health, wealth and joy. A chance to start anew and make amends with the past. According to Hindu scriptures, Yugaadikrit was one of the many names of Lord Vishnu, which means the creator of ages or Yuga. The festival of Ugadi also marks the arrival of the spring season and the beginning of a new era. Therefore, people in south India worship Lords Brahma & Vishnu and seek blessings from the lords for new ideas, new crops, as well as continued happiness, & prosperity in their lives. Before creation must come destruction. But, after the old is gone, something new must rise to take its place. A cycle of creation and destruction and this cycle continues. "Yesmin Krishno divamvyataha, Tasmat eeva pratipannam Kaliyugam". Just as a new age began as Lord Krishna left this world, a time for mankind began again and once more, to shape the world around us to advance to the future. Hold to our principles and convictions and we will be rewarded just as the earth rewards her children for their patience. I am wishing everyone a very happy Ugadi!

Happy Diwali

Diwali, famously known worldwide as the festival of lights. It is one of the biggest and most important holidays of the year. Each region of India marks a different story of Diwali. One of the main stories is of the Day Lord Rama defeated the demon Raavanna and returned to Ayodhya along with his wife Sita and his brother Lakshmana. Another is of the day Lord Krishna defeated the demon Narakasura and freed the people in his kingdom. Other people celebrate the Goddess Lakshmi Devi as she is the Goddess of prosperity, wealth & fertility. A day remembered and celebrated for when good triumphed over evil, light won over darkness, knowledge won over ignorance. A time also to burn clay lamps to line up outside the house to mark the way home after a hard day of work for both the animals and people. It is also a time to put aside past grudges and make peace, to organize reunions and gather with friends and family. A time to celebrate, eat food, and drink together with loved ones. A time for when family and friends cover the streets and buildings in festive lighting and sing and dance to lively songs as well as fire off fireworks and exchange colorful boxes filled with delicacies. I am wishing everyone a very lively, happy, and joyous Diwali!

Home

Home. A place of comfort and belonging. We search for belonging and acceptance. A family, a people who we can depend on and call our own. Yet, if the very people we look to for trust and care are the ones who tear us apart to shreds, who else is there?! From the days of yore, we look and search for the tribe, for the community, for support, and for companionship. Where our heart desires to go, to finally rest after the long, hard days. The world seems so connected, on the other hand, there is a feeling of loneliness, like being on an island stuck far away from the mainland. Stuck in a desert in the middle of nowhere. And yet, we look for that somewhere when we are nowhere. A place of passion, of affection, of joy, of warmth. A tribe, a family, a home. A place where we can find peace, yet our journey continues on.

Loss and Pain

Loss. A pain that is slow, like a dagger through flesh, yet more excruciating and agonizing. A darkness that even the light of the heavens cannot peirce. It is silent and burning, like a slow poison. Though detection is possible, a cure is difficult to find. An agony that leaves a hole where the heart should be. Where one could find light, there is now a shadow, a hidden mist, an opening to a world of regret and guilt. No pleasure can be found, only sorrow. A smile vanquished. In its place, a melancholy look. Time cannot heal all wounds. Some, we live with. Some we must accept. To keep moving, to keep a future.

Sunlit Path

Today, the first rays of sunlight appeared. A beautiful morning starts a beautiful day. A bright welcoming light. With the sun, even the flowers rose. The darkness subsided before the blaze of the first fire. The clouds gave way. The snow and ice have softened to make way. Even the heavens have come out to play. A bright day. A good day. A new day. Time to rise, time to soar. A chance to experience the spring and with it, a chance to see a new choice.

True Love

Her hand has only touched my hand. Yet, her gentle whisper has touched my very soul. Her eyes like the water from the heavens above pierced through the stone that was my heart. Her hand alone made me experience the sacred touch of the snow of Mount Kailash. When she turned, the earth itself turned right and left. She has embraced my body. Like a person caught in a tornado, her hair wrapped itself around my neck. Before the smile of my beloved, even the sun's light is small in comparison. Before her, the sky itself bowed. My mind, body and soul was trapped by her embrace. The time needed to recover from her is a lifetime, no. An eternity. Perhaps this is what true love is.

A Transcending Angel

Your smile makes the moon's light small in comparison. Your warm touch can melt even the coldest of ice. Your heart belongs in the scale of this universe. Your soul, a beautiful transcending angel. Even the waves part when you walk toward them. God has perfected you, my love, as there is no other flower which can match your beauty and power.

A Flower with Strength

You have truly blossomed into a beautiful flower. A flower filled with the beauty of fire. Yet also with the beauty of the first snow. Your voice is a heavenly angel landing on this earth. Your touch is, the snow of mountains that can pierce the heavens. Your anger, a sacred fire that can burn the world. With your smile, the light of the stars come to life. My love, your strength is unparalleled. You are a goddess come to earth in human form. This heart of steel has melted in your presence. What have I done to be blessed with your eternal beauty and love.

www.ingramcontent.com/pod-product-compliance
Lightning Source LLC
Chambersburg PA
CBHW051749130826
49812CB00033B/1071